EMMANUEL JOSEPH

Chronicles of Balance, Pursuing Health, Wealth, and Interpersonal Harmony

Copyright © 2025 by Emmanuel Joseph

All rights reserved. No part of this publication may be reproduced, stored or transmitted in any form or by any means, electronic, mechanical, photocopying, recording, scanning, or otherwise without written permission from the publisher. It is illegal to copy this book, post it to a website, or distribute it by any other means without permission.

First edition

*This book was professionally typeset on Reedsy.
Find out more at reedsy.com*

Contents

1	Chapter 1: The Foundation of Health	1
2	Chapter 2: Wealth Beyond Material Possessions	3
3	Chapter 3: Cultivating Interpersonal Harmony	5
4	Chapter 4: The Intersection of Health and Wealth	7
5	Chapter 5: Building and Maintaining Healthy Relationships	9
6	Chapter 6: The Role of Mindfulness in Balance	11
7	Chapter 7: The Power of Positive Habits	13
8	Chapter 8: Embracing Change and Adaptability	15
9	Chapter 9: The Harmony of Work and Life	17
10	Chapter 10: The Influence of Environment on Balance	19
11	Chapter 11: The Role of Purpose and Passion	21
12	Chapter 12: The Impact of Technology on Balance	23
13	Chapter 13: The Essence of Gratitude	25
14	Chapter 14: The Journey of Lifelong Learning	26
15	Chapter 15: The Legacy of Balance	28

1

Chapter 1: The Foundation of Health

In the pursuit of a balanced life, health forms the cornerstone upon which all other aspects are built. Without a solid foundation of physical and mental well-being, the other pillars—wealth and interpersonal harmony—become unstable and prone to collapse. To understand health in its entirety, one must consider not only the absence of illness but also the presence of vitality, energy, and a sense of purpose. Health is not a static state but a dynamic process that requires continuous nurturing and attention.

Physical health, the most visible aspect of our well-being, demands a proactive approach. Regular exercise, balanced nutrition, and adequate rest are essential components. Exercise not only strengthens the body but also invigorates the mind, reducing stress and enhancing cognitive functions. Nutrition, on the other hand, serves as the fuel for our daily endeavors. A diet rich in diverse nutrients ensures that our body operates at its peak efficiency. Rest, often overlooked in our fast-paced lives, is the period during which our body repairs and rejuvenates itself.

Mental health is equally critical, though often shrouded in stigma and misunderstanding. It encompasses our emotional, psychological, and social well-being. Mental health influences how we think, feel, and act, and it determines how we handle stress, relate to others, and make choices. The pursuit of mental health involves cultivating resilience, practicing mindfulness, and seeking help when needed. It's about acknowledging our emotions, embracing our vulnerabilities, and striving for inner peace.

Ultimately, the foundation of health is holistic. It's an intricate tapestry woven from the threads of physical vitality, mental clarity, and emotional stability. By prioritizing our health, we create a solid base upon which we can build the other essential elements of a balanced life—wealth and interpersonal harmony. The journey toward health is ongoing, demanding consistent effort and dedication. Yet, it's a journey that promises unparalleled rewards, as it paves the way for a life of fulfillment and harmony.

2

Chapter 2: Wealth Beyond Material Possessions

Wealth is often misunderstood as merely the accumulation of material possessions and financial assets. However, true wealth extends far beyond the confines of monetary value. It encompasses a sense of abundance in various aspects of life, including time, relationships, experiences, and personal growth. In the quest for balance, it's essential to redefine wealth to include these broader dimensions that contribute to overall well-being and fulfillment.

Financial stability is undeniably a critical component of wealth. It provides the security and freedom to pursue our passions, support our loved ones, and contribute to our communities. Sound financial management involves budgeting, saving, investing, and making informed decisions that align with our long-term goals. It's about creating a sustainable financial plan that enables us to live comfortably today while preparing for the future.

However, wealth is also measured by the richness of our experiences and the quality of our relationships. Time is a precious commodity, and how we choose to spend it significantly impacts our sense of wealth. Investing in experiences that bring joy, learning, and personal growth can create lasting memories and a deep sense of satisfaction. Cultivating meaningful relationships with family, friends, and colleagues enriches our lives in ways that material possessions never can.

Moreover, personal growth and self-improvement are vital aspects of true wealth. Lifelong learning, acquiring new skills, and pursuing our passions contribute to a sense of accomplishment and purpose. This continuous journey of self-discovery and growth enhances our resilience, adaptability, and overall happiness. By embracing a holistic view of wealth, we create a more balanced and fulfilling life that goes beyond mere financial success.

3

Chapter 3: Cultivating Interpersonal Harmony

Interpersonal harmony is the art of nurturing positive, respectful, and meaningful relationships with others. It is rooted in empathy, communication, and understanding. In a world where individualism often prevails, cultivating harmony in our interactions with others can transform our lives and create a supportive and enriching community.

Effective communication is the cornerstone of interpersonal harmony. It involves not only expressing our thoughts and feelings clearly but also actively listening to others. Listening with empathy and an open mind fosters mutual understanding and trust. It allows us to appreciate different perspectives and find common ground, even in the face of disagreements. By practicing active listening, we show others that we value their opinions and experiences.

Empathy, the ability to understand and share the feelings of others, is essential for building strong and harmonious relationships. It requires us to put ourselves in others' shoes and consider their emotions and experiences. Empathy encourages compassion, kindness, and patience, helping us navigate conflicts and challenges with grace. By developing our empathetic abilities, we create a more supportive and connected community.

Respect for others is another critical element of interpersonal harmony. It involves acknowledging and valuing each person's unique qualities, experiences, and contributions. Respectful interactions promote a sense of belonging and self-worth, fostering positive relationships and a harmonious environment. By treating others with respect, we create a culture of inclusivity and mutual support.

Interpersonal harmony is an ongoing journey that requires continuous effort and commitment. It involves self-awareness, emotional intelligence, and a willingness to grow and adapt. By prioritizing harmony in our relationships, we enhance our overall well-being and contribute to a more balanced and fulfilling life.

4

Chapter 4: The Intersection of Health and Wealth

The relationship between health and wealth is intricate and symbiotic. A healthy individual is more likely to be productive, make informed decisions, and pursue opportunities that enhance their financial stability. Conversely, financial security provides the means to access quality healthcare, nutritious food, and opportunities for physical and mental well-being. Understanding this interplay is crucial for achieving a balanced and fulfilling life.

One of the key intersections between health and wealth is stress management. Financial stress can have severe implications for both physical and mental health, leading to conditions such as hypertension, anxiety, and depression. Effective financial planning and budgeting can alleviate this stress, providing peace of mind and improving overall well-being. By managing our finances wisely, we reduce the burden of financial worries and create a more stable foundation for our health.

Investment in health is another critical aspect of the health-wealth relationship. Prioritizing spending on preventive healthcare, regular exercise, and nutritious food can lead to long-term savings by reducing medical expenses and enhancing productivity. For example, maintaining a healthy lifestyle can prevent chronic diseases that are costly to treat. Thus, viewing health as an investment, rather than an expense, is essential for long-term wealth accumulation and preservation.

Moreover, health and wealth intersect in the realm of work-life balance. Overworking in pursuit of financial success can take a toll on one's health, leading to burnout and decreased productivity. Striking a balance between work and personal life is crucial for maintaining both health and financial stability. It involves setting boundaries, prioritizing self-care, and ensuring that time is allocated for rest, relaxation, and leisure activities. By achieving a harmonious balance, we enhance our overall quality of life and sustain our capacity for wealth generation.

5

Chapter 5: Building and Maintaining Healthy Relationships

Healthy relationships are fundamental to a balanced life, contributing to our emotional well-being, sense of belonging, and overall happiness. Building and maintaining these relationships requires effort, communication, and mutual respect. Whether with family, friends, or colleagues, the quality of our relationships significantly impacts our mental and emotional health.

Trust is the foundation of any healthy relationship. It involves being reliable, honest, and consistent in our actions and words. Trust is built over time through shared experiences and mutual support. By fostering trust, we create a safe and secure environment where individuals feel valued and respected.

Effective communication is another vital component of healthy relationships. It involves not only expressing our thoughts and feelings clearly but also listening actively and empathetically. Communication should be open, honest, and respectful, allowing for the expression of emotions and the resolution of conflicts. By improving our communication skills, we enhance our ability to connect with others and strengthen our relationships.

Respect and appreciation are also essential for nurturing healthy relationships. Recognizing and valuing each person's unique qualities and contributions fosters a sense of belonging and self-worth. Showing gratitude, offering encouragement, and celebrating achievements create a positive and supportive environment. By practicing respect and appreciation, we cultivate relationships that are enriching and fulfilling.

Maintaining healthy relationships also requires setting boundaries and managing conflicts effectively. Boundaries help us protect our well-being and ensure that our needs are met. They involve understanding our limits and communicating them clearly to others. Conflict is inevitable in any relationship, but how we handle it determines its impact. Approaching conflicts with empathy, understanding, and a willingness to compromise helps resolve issues constructively and strengthens the relationship.

6

Chapter 6: The Role of Mindfulness in Balance

Mindfulness, the practice of being present and fully engaged in the moment, plays a crucial role in achieving balance in life. It helps us manage stress, improve mental clarity, and enhance our overall well-being. By incorporating mindfulness into our daily routines, we cultivate a sense of awareness and appreciation for the present moment.

One of the primary benefits of mindfulness is stress reduction. By focusing on the present moment, we can detach from past regrets and future anxieties. Mindfulness techniques, such as meditation, deep breathing, and mindful walking, help calm the mind and reduce the physiological effects of stress. By practicing mindfulness regularly, we develop resilience and a greater capacity to handle life's challenges.

Mindfulness also enhances mental clarity and focus. By training our minds to stay present, we improve our ability to concentrate and make thoughtful decisions. Mindfulness helps us become more aware of our thoughts and emotions, allowing us to respond to situations with greater intention and composure. This heightened awareness improves our problem-solving skills and promotes a more balanced and thoughtful approach to life.

Incorporating mindfulness into our daily lives also enhances our relationships and interactions with others. By being fully present in our conversations and activities, we show others that we value and respect their time and presence. Mindfulness fosters empathy, active listening, and genuine connection, strengthening our bonds with others. It also helps us manage conflicts and communicate more effectively.

Ultimately, mindfulness encourages a deeper appreciation for the present moment and the simple joys of life. It reminds us to savor our experiences, whether it's a beautiful sunset, a heartfelt conversation, or a moment of quiet reflection. By embracing mindfulness, we cultivate a sense of gratitude and fulfillment, contributing to a more balanced and harmonious life.

7

Chapter 7: The Power of Positive Habits

Positive habits are the building blocks of a balanced and fulfilling life. They shape our daily routines, influence our behavior, and determine our long-term success and well-being. By cultivating positive habits, we create a framework for achieving our goals and maintaining a harmonious lifestyle.

The first step in developing positive habits is identifying the behaviors that align with our values and aspirations. These might include regular exercise, healthy eating, mindfulness practices, and time management. Once identified, it's important to integrate these habits into our daily routines. Consistency is key—small, incremental changes repeated over time lead to significant, lasting transformations.

Accountability plays a crucial role in habit formation. Sharing our goals with others and seeking support from friends, family, or a community can help us stay motivated and committed. Accountability partners provide encouragement, feedback, and a sense of camaraderie, making the journey of habit formation more enjoyable and sustainable.

It's also essential to be patient and compassionate with ourselves during this process. Forming new habits takes time and effort, and setbacks are a natural part of the journey. Instead of being discouraged by occasional slip-ups, we should view them as opportunities for learning and growth. By maintaining a positive mindset and celebrating our progress, we stay motivated and resilient.

8

Chapter 8: Embracing Change and Adaptability

Change is an inevitable part of life, and our ability to adapt to it significantly impacts our overall balance and well-being. Embracing change with an open mind and a flexible attitude allows us to navigate life's uncertainties and challenges with grace and resilience.

One of the keys to embracing change is developing a growth mindset. This mindset views challenges and setbacks as opportunities for learning and growth rather than as insurmountable obstacles. By adopting a growth mindset, we become more adaptable and open to new experiences, enhancing our ability to thrive in a constantly changing world.

Another important aspect of adaptability is cultivating resilience. Resilience involves the ability to bounce back from adversity and maintain a positive outlook despite difficulties. Building resilience requires self-awareness, emotional regulation, and a strong support system. Practices such as mindfulness, self-care, and seeking social support can enhance our resilience and help us navigate change more effectively.

Embracing change also involves being proactive and taking control of the aspects of our lives that we can influence. This might include setting goals, planning for the future, and continuously seeking opportunities for personal and professional growth. By taking an active role in shaping our lives, we become more empowered and capable of handling change.

9

Chapter 9: The Harmony of Work and Life

Achieving a harmonious balance between work and personal life is essential for overall well-being and fulfillment. The demands of work can often spill over into our personal lives, leading to stress, burnout, and strained relationships. Striking a balance requires intentional effort and a commitment to prioritizing our well-being.

One of the keys to work-life harmony is setting clear boundaries. This involves defining specific times and spaces for work and personal activities and adhering to these boundaries consistently. By establishing limits, we create a clear separation between work and personal life, allowing us to fully engage in and enjoy each aspect.

Time management is another crucial component of work-life harmony. Effective time management involves prioritizing tasks, setting realistic goals, and eliminating distractions. By organizing our time efficiently, we can accomplish our work responsibilities while ensuring that we have time for personal activities, relaxation, and self-care.

Self-care is essential for maintaining work-life harmony. It involves taking time to nurture our physical, mental, and emotional well-being. Self-care practices might include exercise, meditation, hobbies, spending time with loved ones, and taking breaks to recharge. By prioritizing self-care, we enhance our capacity to handle work demands and maintain a balanced and fulfilling life.

10

Chapter 10: The Influence of Environment on Balance

Our environment plays a significant role in shaping our well-being and sense of balance. The spaces we inhabit, the people we interact with, and the cultural and social contexts we navigate all influence our physical and mental health. Creating a supportive and harmonious environment is crucial for achieving and maintaining balance.

A key aspect of a supportive environment is the physical space we occupy. Our homes, workplaces, and recreational areas should be designed to promote health, comfort, and productivity. This might involve organizing our spaces to reduce clutter, incorporating elements of nature, and ensuring adequate lighting and ventilation. A well-designed environment enhances our mood, energy levels, and overall well-being.

Social interactions are another important component of our environment. Surrounding ourselves with positive, supportive, and like-minded individuals fosters a sense of belonging and mutual support. Engaging in meaningful social activities and building strong relationships contribute to our emotional well-being and create a sense of community.

Cultural and social contexts also influence our sense of balance. The values, norms, and expectations of the societies we live in shape our behavior and perceptions. Being aware of these influences and aligning our actions with our values and goals can help us navigate social pressures and maintain a balanced life.

11

Chapter 11: The Role of Purpose and Passion

Living a life of purpose and passion is essential for achieving balance and fulfillment. Purpose gives our lives meaning and direction, while passion fuels our enthusiasm and motivation. Together, they create a sense of alignment and drive that propels us toward our goals and aspirations.

Finding our purpose involves exploring our values, strengths, and interests. It requires self-reflection and a willingness to ask deep, meaningful questions about what truly matters to us. Purpose can be found in various aspects of life, such as our careers, relationships, hobbies, and contributions to society. By identifying and pursuing our purpose, we create a sense of fulfillment and satisfaction that transcends material success.

Passion, on the other hand, is the energy and excitement that comes from engaging in activities we love. It ignites our creativity, enhances our performance, and brings joy to our lives. Cultivating passion involves exploring new interests, taking risks, and embracing opportunities for growth and learning. By pursuing our passions, we infuse our lives with vitality and enthusiasm.

When purpose and passion align, we experience a profound sense of harmony and balance. Our actions become meaningful and intentional, and we are driven by a deep sense of fulfillment. By integrating purpose and passion into our lives, we create a holistic and balanced approach to well-being.

12

Chapter 12: The Impact of Technology on Balance

Technology has become an integral part of modern life, shaping how we communicate, work, and access information. While technology offers numerous benefits, it also presents challenges to achieving balance. Managing our relationship with technology is essential for maintaining well-being and harmony in our lives.

One of the key challenges of technology is the constant connectivity and information overload it creates. The barrage of notifications, emails, and social media updates can lead to stress, distraction, and reduced productivity. Establishing boundaries with technology, such as setting specific times for checking emails and social media, can help mitigate its negative impact. By creating tech-free zones and moments, we reclaim our time and mental space for more meaningful activities.

Technology also influences our physical health. Prolonged screen time can lead to eye strain, poor posture, and sedentary behavior. To counteract these effects, it's important to incorporate regular breaks, physical activity, and ergonomic practices into our daily routines. By balancing screen time with physical movement and outdoor activities, we enhance our overall well-being.

On the positive side, technology offers valuable tools for enhancing our health, wealth, and interpersonal harmony. Fitness apps, online learning platforms, and virtual communication tools provide opportunities for personal growth, financial management, and social connection. By using technology mindfully and intentionally, we can harness its benefits while minimizing its drawbacks.

13

Chapter 13: The Essence of Gratitude

Gratitude is a powerful practice that enhances our overall well-being and sense of balance. It involves recognizing and appreciating the positive aspects of our lives, no matter how big or small. Cultivating gratitude shifts our focus from what we lack to what we have, fostering a sense of abundance and contentment.

One of the simplest ways to practice gratitude is by keeping a gratitude journal. Each day, take a few moments to write down things you are thankful for. These can range from basic necessities to meaningful experiences and relationships. By regularly reflecting on the positives in our lives, we cultivate a mindset of appreciation and joy.

Gratitude also extends to our interactions with others. Expressing gratitude to those who have positively impacted our lives strengthens our relationships and fosters a sense of connection. Simple acts of kindness and appreciation, such as saying thank you or writing a heartfelt note, create a ripple effect of positivity and harmony.

Moreover, practicing gratitude enhances our resilience and ability to cope with challenges. It shifts our perspective, helping us find silver linings and opportunities for growth in difficult situations. By focusing on the positives, we build emotional strength and maintain a balanced outlook on life.

14

Chapter 14: The Journey of Lifelong Learning

L ifelong learning is a cornerstone of personal growth and balance. It involves continuously seeking knowledge, skills, and experiences that enrich our lives and expand our horizons. Embracing a mindset of curiosity and openness to learning enhances our adaptability, creativity, and overall well-being.

Lifelong learning can take many forms, from formal education and professional development to self-directed exploration and hobbies. It includes reading books, attending workshops, taking online courses, and engaging in activities that challenge and stimulate our minds. By prioritizing learning, we stay intellectually engaged and motivated.

In addition to acquiring new knowledge, lifelong learning also involves unlearning and relearning. It requires us to question assumptions, challenge biases, and adapt to new information and perspectives. This process of continuous growth fosters critical thinking and enhances our ability to navigate an ever-changing world.

Furthermore, lifelong learning enriches our personal and professional lives. It opens doors to new opportunities, enhances our skills and competencies, and deepens our understanding of ourselves and the world around us. By committing to lifelong learning, we cultivate a sense of purpose, fulfillment,

CHAPTER 14: THE JOURNEY OF LIFELONG LEARNING

and balance.

15

Chapter 15: The Legacy of Balance

As we conclude our journey through the chronicles of balance, it's important to reflect on the legacy we leave behind. Living a balanced life is not only about personal fulfillment but also about making a positive impact on others and the world. Our actions, values, and contributions shape the legacy we create.

One of the ways we leave a lasting legacy is through the relationships we build. The love, support, and kindness we offer to others create a ripple effect that extends beyond our lifetime. By fostering meaningful connections and nurturing those around us, we contribute to a more harmonious and compassionate world.

Our contributions to society also form an essential part of our legacy. Whether through our careers, volunteer work, or creative endeavors, we have the power to make a difference. By aligning our actions with our values and passions, we leave a positive mark on the world and inspire others to do the same.

Lastly, our legacy is reflected in the way we live our lives. By embodying the principles of health, wealth, and interpersonal harmony, we serve as role models for others. Our journey of balance becomes a source of inspiration and guidance for future generations.

In a world that constantly demands more from us, finding balance can seem like an elusive dream. "**Chronicles of Balance: Pursuing Health,**

CHAPTER 15: THE LEGACY OF BALANCE

Wealth, and Interpersonal Harmony" is a transformative journey through the intricate dance of health, wealth, and interpersonal relationships. This book delves deep into the art of living a balanced life, offering practical insights and wisdom to help you achieve holistic well-being.

From laying the foundation of physical and mental health to redefining wealth beyond material possessions, each chapter provides a fresh perspective on what it means to live a fulfilling life. Discover the power of positive habits, the role of mindfulness, and the impact of technology on our sense of balance. Learn to embrace change, cultivate resilience, and find harmony between work and life.

Through engaging narratives and thought-provoking reflections, "Chronicles of Balance" invites you to explore the essence of purpose, passion, and gratitude. It encourages you to build and maintain healthy relationships, invest in lifelong learning, and create a legacy of balance that extends beyond your own life.

Whether you're seeking to improve your health, enhance your financial well-being, or strengthen your interpersonal connections, this book is your guide to a harmonious and fulfilling life. Embark on this journey of balance and discover the profound rewards of pursuing health, wealth, and interpersonal harmony.

www.ingramcontent.com/pod-product-compliance
Lightning Source LLC
LaVergne TN
LVHW020740090526
838202LV00057BA/6139